Lighting Candles 2

Another 31 Day Devotional to Inspire a Closer relationship with God

T Lee Sizemore

This is a work of non-fiction.
Text and illustrations are copyrighted by
T Lee Sizemore, DVM, RN ©2019

Library of Congress Control Number: 2019911047
All rights reserved.

No part of this book may be
reproduced, transmitted, or stored in an
information retrieval
system in any form or by any means,
graphic, electronic, or mechanical without prior
written permission from the author.

First Edition 2020
Printed in the United States of America
A 2 Z Press LLC
PO Box 582
Deleon Springs, FL 32130
bestlittleonlinebookstore.com
sizemore3630@aol.com
440-241-3126
ISBN: 978-1-946908-72-8

Dedication

***This book is dedicated to her father,
Edwin Sizemore.
I thank him for believing for and
praying for me to have faith.***

Day 1- Personal Relationship

Being born a long time ago makes me feel pretty old - especially when I meet someone born in 2002. Can you imagine not knowing who Fonzi is? Or not having seen the Monkies live on Ed Sullivan? Who's Ed Sullivan some ask? Yes, I get it. I used to wonder what it was like in the 1920's. There are those who remember.

That brings me to my current blog. I recently learned of the 1973 film *Sleeper*. I have never seen the film, but understand that in the movie, Woody Allen plays a character who wakes up 200 years after being frozen in a scientific experiment. He is given a stack of photographs from our century to identify. This prompts a series of hilarious one-liners. I'll bet everyone who has ever looked at old photos can relate. In *Sleeper*, one of the photos was of the late Billy Graham. Woody Allen pauses, then says, "Billy Graham...claimed to have a personal relationship with God." The audience, of course, cracks up. That is how absurd the idea sounds to many people. Especially in this 'new' age.

I think it's pretty sad to think a relationship with God is absurd. I had a co-worker who wrote an email to my boss stating I was mentally ill for claiming to have a relationship with the Living God. The Bible outlines how Jesus came to us, was born a Baby, lived, did many miracles and taught people just like us, died, and rose from the grave so *we* could have a personal relationship with Him. The dictionary defines personal as 'individual, private, as one's own, intended for use by one person.'

There are many questions facing us today. Do we walk this walk alone? Is there an unseen Providence? Are our steps really ordered by the Lord? (Proverbs 20.24) Should we pray about things or just trust medication or the 'new way' of making ourselves feel valuable and with purpose? Michael W. Smith sings a song about Providence. Some of the words are, "The Hand of Providence, Oh, it's evident, we could never make it on our own." I see God in everything.

I know it is God's intent that everyone know Him in a special and personal way - not in imagination about what He is like and Who He is, but in a real and personal way. In a way that pictures of us will prompt the on-looker to say, 'They claimed to have a personal relationship with God.' What a nice thing to say about someone.

Write how you came to know Jesus. Are you finding is 'exhilarating?' Describe your experience.

Day 2 – Everything

Don't we all love those days when everything goes right. Work is good, family is happy, lines at the store are short, you hit all the lights green, no flat tire today, you won a scratch off! Wow, life doesn't get better. It is easy at these times - when things seem to go smoothly and our performance seems adequate - to think we are on God's A-list and must be loved and valued.

Then there are those not-so-great days. Bad news at work, family struggling, bills mounting, taxes due,- and on and on the list may go. It is these days - when we feel discouraged, we may tend to think we are not on God's "A-list." The truth is we are on God's A -list each and every day. No matter how many mistakes we make or bad days we have, God is always our Father.

The 'amazing' thing is that our lives have always been and always will be about grace. Amazing Grace. The Bible tells us "It is by grace (God's undeserved favor) that we are saved from any punishment or judgment and made partakers of

Christ's salvation....it is a gift from God." We start in grace, we walk every day in grace, and we end our lives on this side of heaven because of grace. (Ephesians 2.7-10)

Another special part of the Bible encourages me more of how amazing grace is - 2 Corinthians 7-11 confirms that Moses' face shown so much with the Glory of God when he came from Sinai with the law they had to put a veil over his face. They could not look at the brilliance. Now the law is passed - God's Word continues to ask us 'How much more glory is there in grace- that will never pass away?' These Words touched my heart in such a real and personal way when I needed to realize the magnificence of His grace to me and everyone.

Sometimes I judge others harshly. I see them as unable to be more like God, happier, more positive, less 'human' to be honest. Frail. Failing to be perfect. Easy to point fingers at others when I should be pointing them at myself for the many mistakes I make each day. Then, I see God again as the Giver of Amazing Grace to me and the ones I judge incorrectly. God does not see them the tainted way I do.

No matter how many difficult days we have, God is in each and every moment. God is Love and Love bears all things, believes all things, hopes all things, endures all things. Love NEVER fails. (1 Corinthians 13) And we have Jesus - our High Priest - who is touched with the feeling of our infirmity - any inability to cope, any weakness, and inherent flaws - anything we struggle with. (Hebrews 4.15) Isn't it wonderful that we have a Savior Who knows everything about us - the good, the bad, and the ugly- , loves us with an everlasting love beyond our comprehension, does not hold our shortcomings against us, and wants to have us as His children. It truly is Amazing Grace.

Write how you feel about prayer. Who is on your list of prayer concerns? Are you developing a prayer life?

Day 3 - Prayer

Beside Jesus, the Holy Spirit, and God, my favorite person in the Bible is Paul. At first, Paul was not a believer and participated in the execution of believers. He was struck down on the road to Damascus by God Himself - an encounter that led to his conversion to Christianity. He was temporarily blinded by the incident as well as Divinely commissioned to the service of Christ.

Paul had visions and dreams given by the Holy Spirit, been raised to the third heaven and heard unutterable things, survived beatings that should have killed him, had prison chains snapped by an earthquake, received 39 lashes 5 times from the Jews, was beaten by the Romans 3 times, was stoned by his enemies once, was shipwrecked 3 times, spent a night and day on the open sea, and on frequent journeys, faced dangers from rivers, robbers, his own people, the non-Jewish people, dangers in the city, open country, sea, and false brothers. Paul faced labor and hardship, many sleepless nights, hunger and thirst as well as went without food often and was often cold and lacked clothing. Paul goes on to say, not to mention other things - he had daily pressure on him, had to care for all the churches and his hands had been the gloves of God in countless wonders. (2 Corinthians 11.21-28) WOW! and all this never diminished his faith in the Living God.

I am amazed by the faith of Paul. What I am also amazed by is that of all the writers of Divine Scripture, Paul was inspired to write about prayer more than any other. In searching the Holman Christian Standard Bible, I discovered that in the letters written, Paul talks about prayer 26 times. In addition, he mentions words meaning prayer - supplication and intercession - 27 times. This man - who had been tortured on many occasions - is obsessed with prayer. So should we be. Why was he obsessed with prayer?

Prayer is the mystery of Christianity and powerful. In search of 'pray' and 'prayer' in the Holman Christian Standard Bible, prayer is referenced 356 times in the entire Bible. Prayer for life, fertility, success, finances, healing, winning battles, thankfulness, and many more reasons. These have given us the example to not just stand by and let 'whatever happens, happen.'
Whatever need we or our loved ones have, we can pray.
Prayer matters everything. Our lives and the lives of the ones we love are shaped and influenced by our prayers. God is listening. It does not matter the form our prayers take or the posture we take when praying, it just matters that we pray - and

pray at all times for all things. Pray for your family, pray for your neighbors, pray for your teachers, pray for the ones stranded on the road, the homeless, the needy. Pray for healing and deliverance, pray for salvation of our loved ones. Pray, pray, pray.

Write how you make time each day for Bible reading and how you find God in that time.

_____
_____
_____
_____
_____
_____
_____
_____
_____
_____
_____
_____
_____
_____
_____
_____
_____
_____
_____
_____
_____
_____
_____

Day 4 – Peddling

I love this painting. It is pure chaos. Just like life sometimes. I know people who seem to claim they have an answer for everything. I, however, am not one of them.

I am not certain how this happened, but recently I engaged in debate with two friends about who has experienced the most struggle in life. Weird debate, right? Both shared their stories with me and I wept. I lost the debates. It amazes me how those around me are brave enough to continue each day despite the hardships they endured as children and young adults. Stories of loss of parents through suicide, abandonment as young children, physical and emotional abuse, and more.

Sometimes people feel there is no God because of all that seems to be wrong in the world. I admit I don't have all the answers. I don't think anyone will ever be able to make sense of things that just don't make sense.

I don't have an answer for why children get

cancer, why mothers die young leaving their families, why houses burn down or floods happen. Why children are abducted, why murder happens as well as war. Why we choose to persecute those not like us. All the things that don't make sense in life do not shake my belief in a God that loves us and promises to give beauty for ashes. (Isaiah 61.3) I have always held the opinion we have the opportunity to make our pain our pathway to God. I believe we can know Him a way we would never have been able to know Him without the pain that seems to be destroying our happiness.

In the midst of everything, He is always the Answer to everything. Even what does not make sense. He is still Good and Loving and Able to get us through everything and make us able to help those around us. I realized those that struggle with diabetes campaign passionately about diabetes. Those that have lost a loved one to Alzheimer's passionately campaign for this disorder. Why does it take pain to move us to help those around us? I am not certain, however, the truth is I am passionate about the struggles I have faced in my quest to help those that also struggle with the same.

In the Bible, Job demands to talk to God. Job wants to tell God how unjust He has been and how the suffering has been greater than he was able to bear. God does talk to Job and gently asks Job if he created all we see around us? Are we smarter than God? No. He put all the world together, He knows all the past, present, and future events, He created the horse and the whale, and He is smarter, kinder, more loving, more creative, more everything than we can ever be. In the end of all things, we will understand. I suppose at that time, explanations will not even be an issue any longer.

I do not want to be accused of peddling easy answers to difficult questions, but for now, I pray we put our hands in the Hand of the Living God and continue to walk through each day, giving Him our struggles, our dreams, our happiness, our everything. We can trust the Man Who died for us so we can have beauty for the ashes we feel have come to us in this life.

Write how you feel you are surrendering to Jesus and finding your life as you lose it in Him.

_____
_____
_____
_____
_____
_____
_____
_____
_____
_____
_____
_____
_____
_____
_____
_____

Day 5 - Mercy

I love the French language because it sounds so soft and romantic. For instance, the word 'merci' is sweet to me. When the Olympics were in France, I heard everyone on television saying, 'merci.' I wished I was there.

Merci - thank you. What a lovely translation. The word 'merci' also reminds me of the word 'mercy' - one of my other favorite words in English for an incredible gift God gives to me and everyone.

I think the word mercy is overused at times and poorly understood. I already said it is an incredible gift, but it seems I am stunned when I think about mercy, so I say it again. I want to really absorb the rich meaning and impact mercy has on my life and the life of the ones I love. In Webster's, we find the meaning of the word 'mercy' to include 'the discretionary power of a Judge to pardon someone - compassion shown to an offender.' This is ok, but not the deep and special meaning of the word to me. The faith filled meaning of the word is that God show us mercy - He pardons us and loves us even when we are not lovable.

I once heard the story of a woman whose son was sentenced to death for crimes he had committed. His mother pled for his life. She cried out, "Have mercy on my son." The leader declared, "Your son does not deserve mercy!" She replied, "If he deserved it, it would not be mercy." The leader was so touched by the woman's words that he released the man.

Even though I am not a criminal sentenced to death in this life, I am a sinful woman who lives in a sinful world and at one time I was sentenced to eternal death. I did not and do not 'deserve' mercy. It is because of the mercy of God that I am alive today because I was in danger of ending my life over 30 years ago. Because of the mercy and grace of the Living God, I am physically alive as well as spiritually alive. I am 'thankful.' Thankful for mercy. I guess one could say merci for mercy. My heart is deeply touched by the mercy of God, so it allows me to see His mercy for the ones around me.

Each day I try to live the life I want God to be proud of, but I make many mistakes. Sometimes those around me are flawed and do things that are hurtful to themselves and others and me. God's mercy is for all the things we cannot seem to do right every moment of every day. It is an awesome gift that is beyond my comprehension at times. No matter how many times we fail each day, He picks us up, dusts us off, and continues down the road with us.

Lamentations 3.22-23 tells us, "the steadfast love of the Lord never ceases, His mercies never come to an end, they are new every morning, great is His faithfulness." Praise Him for all His wonderful gifts.

Who is He to you? Why is He 'this' to you? Do you want Him to be more and in what way?

_____
_____
_____
_____
_____
_____
_____
_____
_____
_____
_____
_____
_____
_____
_____
_____
_____
_____
_____
_____
_____
_____

Day 6 – Love, Again

Recently, I heard a really cute story about children writing notes to God - One little girl wrote, 'Dear God, I'll bet it's very hard for You to love all of everybody in the whole world. There are only four people in our family and I can never do it.'

I can relate. Sometimes it's easier to love in imagination than in reality. It's easier to love those who are nice and co-operative with us. God instructs us to love and Romans 5.5 tells me '….the love of God is shed abroad in our hearts by the Holy Ghost which is given unto us.' It is a gift from God to help us love our families and others. I cannot help but wonder why I it's now so easy so much all the time.

I know from personal experience that it can be difficult to love and the difficult are difficult to love. If only they made it easier to love them! But, I have realized something others have known for many years - the wretched, weak, ornery, addicted, contrary, difficult to love people need and want love too. I don't think they realize how much they need it and want it, but they do.

I used to think that loving someone would make a difference. It makes some difference, it has to, it's love. But perhaps it does not the difference *I* want it to make - to make them easier to love, less difficult to reach, more healed, less problematic, and, to be honest, more perfect. I excuse all my difficulties though and I realize I do that. I want others to love me even when I am not easy to love.

So, what does one do? Philippians 4.13 continually reminds me that 'I can do all things through Christ Who strengthens me.' It is tiring, but finding out what makes someone feel loved and special and trying to do that is how I try to show that I do love them. And prayer - not as a last resort - but as a first resort. Prayer for the ones we love and prayer for guidance in our lives to be able to show them love.

Love makes us feel valuable and worthy and not defective. If someone loves us, we must be something - something and not *nothing*. Sometimes when others talk about God loving me *anyway* - even though I am a schmuck, and don't obey and don't deserve and are full of faults, - it sort of makes me think He doesn't really love me, He is just stuck with me as the imperfect being I am that no one else can love, so He has to. This is not really true.

God really thinks we are special and valuable and talented and all the things we secretly hope we are and worthy of His and others' love. He treasures us and knows everything that makes us happy and sad. He knows everything we need and wants to be 'Our Shepherd, so we do not lack.' Psalm 23.1. He loves us with an 'everlasting love.' Jeremiah 31.3.

Is there someone who needs your love and isn't perfect?

Day 7 – My Easy Load

There are days I just don't know how I am going to get it all done - work, deadlines, visiting friends in nursing homes, caring for the home, pets, etc. Stress is a word. It seems I have a heavier 'cross' to carry than others. At moments, I am not sure I can bear up under the strain of everything and if someone adds one more thing to my already overloaded schedule, I feel I may just have some bad moments.

I look around and so many others seem to have it easy. They have enough money, enough time, happy families, and on and on. They do not seem to struggle much. I guess if I knew everything, I may think differently. It doesn't take long to know everyone has concerns.

A friend shared a little story with me, a story of a girl who felt her 'cross' was heavier than those around her. When she slept, she was taken to a large room filled with crosses. There were large crosses and jewel adorned crosses and many others. In the corner was a small, plain cross. When the girl saw this little cross, she said, "I would like that one. I think I can manage that one small cross in the corner." It was then she was then told that was the cross she had been carrying all along. This humbles me.

I ask God to show me my easy load as I watch others caring for disabled children, elderly family members struggling with dementia and other medical conditions, those living on small incomes, veterans returning with emotional concerns, and many other struggles.

I only need to walk the hallways of a hospital to see the faces of those worrying for the ones they love and those who have been given life changing test results. I only need walk the halls of detox centers to see the empty faces of those who do not know how to recover from addictions. I only need walk the streets to see the homeless and those who are lonely. I only need to visit the closest food bank to see ones who struggle to feed their children. I only need to take time to listen to others share with me about losing family when they were young, being raised by single moms, watching other families love each other and wondering why their family is different.

And when I do, my easy load no longer seems to be so overwhelming. I want to be able to share with anyone struggling how Jesus knows their path and all they face each day and does not disregard them in any way (Isaiah 40.27) but wants to help in every way, every day. And God wants me to help others as much as I am able to make their load a little lighter.

Does someone need your forgiveness? Do you need to forgive someone? Write how you are forgiving all things God is bringing to your attention.

Day 8 – Another Day, Another Miracle

I am a terrible cook, but I love to eat. Especially good food. Especially when someone else is an excellent cook and has prepared something wonderful. Sometimes when I eat, I am so full I do not think I will ever eat again - or at least not for the next few days. But, in a few hours, I am hungry again.

I am reminded of the beloved Lord's prayer that asks God to 'give us this day our daily bread.' (Matthew 6.11) When God's people wandered in the wilderness, they were given daily manna - the bread from heaven (Exodus 16). Just as we need our daily bread to sustain our bodies, we need are daily Bread of Heaven to sustain our spirits and give us life. Each day we need a fresh encounter with God. Just as we cannot rely on yesterdays meals to sustain us today, we cannot rely on yesterday's encounters to be all we need from God. God wants to do a 'new thing' for us each and every day.

Elizabeth Taylor played Velvet Brown in the

movie, "National Velvet." In the movie, she feels guilty asking for 'more.' She feels she is asking for 'more than her share.' I think as believers, we imagine we can exhaust God's good will and His answers to prayers. Another day, another miracle I say. It is impossible to exhaust Him or His resources.

The Bible tell us 'the steadfast love of the Lord never ceases, His mercies never come to an end, they are new every morning, great is His faithfulness' (Lamentations 3.22-23).

I love the words to the poem made into song by Annie Johnson Flint "He Giveth More Grace."

He giveth more grace when the burdens grow greater,
He sendeth more strength when the labors increase;
To added affliction He addeth His mercy;
To multiplied trials, His multiplied peace.
When we have exhausted our store of endurance,
When our strength has failed ere the day is half done,
When we reach the end of our hoarded resources,
Our Father's full giving is only begun.
Fear not that thy need shall exceed His provision,
Our God ever yearns His resources to share;
Lean hard on the arm everlasting, availing;
The Father both thee and thy load will upbear.
His love has no limit; His grace has no measure.
His pow'r has no boundary known unto men;

For out of His infinite riches in Jesus, He giveth, and giveth, and giveth again!

I am so thankful for a God that has endless resources and He giveth and giveth and giveth again. He is our Loving Heavenly Father Who wants to supply our every need and be everything to us.

Write how you protect yourself from being 'tricked.' And how you hold to God's Words.

Day 9 – Do You Want

There is a story in the Bible I have always found interesting. It is - *"Some time later, Jesus went up to Jerusalem ... Now there is in Jerusalem near the Sheep Gate a pool, ... Here a great number of disabled people used to lie -- the blind, the lame, the paralyzed. One who was there had been an invalid for **thirty-eight** years. When Jesus saw him lying there and learned that he had been in this condition for a long time, He asked him, 'Do you want to get well?'" John 5.1-6*

I always wondered why Jesus asked the man *if* he wanted to get well? What kind of a question is this? It has always seemed odd to me that someone who has been 'not well' - especially for 38 years - just may not want to 'get well.' When I analyze it, I think perhaps the man never imagined he could be well. Perhaps he was used to being 'not well' and did not know how he would be if he were well because being 'not well' was all he ever knew. Perhaps he did not think it was even possible to be well - for many reasons. Maybe his illness was incurable, maybe the time he had been ill discouraged him, or maybe other reasons.

I have been very lucky to know God and been healed by Him. About thirty years ago, I suffered from a great depression that caused me to want to end my life. I did not know why I was depressed and the condition continued for five years with no hope of being well or free from the depression. I did not know where to turn and no one I knew seemed to know what was wrong with me and why I was suffering so badly.

The Bible states, "My people perish for lack of knowledge.." (Hosea 4.6) This told me that there was something I did not know that was causing my pain and suffering. I began to search for the reasons and read and availed myself to the help that is in books I read and meetings I attended. I discovered the 'punishment necessary for me to have peace was placed on my Savior the day they crucified Him...' (Isaiah 53.5). He provided my peace with His sacrifice.

I had problems that were causing me harm, but I had been in the behavior patterns so long, not only did I not even realize how damaging the patterns were, change was uncomfortable, frightening, and difficult to say the least. But, if I was going to live and 'be well,' I had to change what I was doing to be healed. I obeyed God and the depression left without medication or hospitalization and has not been back in thirty years.

I am not perfect and struggle every day to make my Father proud of me and show Him how thankful I am that He saved my life. He assures me that His love is Everlasting and He in Unconditional Love and Acceptance. I see others struggling with similar things, but when I try to share, it seems to me they do not 'want to be well.' This confuses me. When I struggled and found an answer, I was elated. I hope if you struggle with addiction, depression, anxiety, negative behaviors or any other struggle, you find your answers and realize God is always the Answer to all our struggles.

Write if you have fear. What about?

_____
_____
_____
_____
_____
_____
_____
_____
_____
_____
_____
_____
_____
_____
_____
_____
_____
_____

Day 10 – A Cup of Cold Water

When I lived in Ohio, I admit I never drank the daily recommended eight eight ounce glasses of water. However, in Florida, it seems I cannot get enough. The temperatures and humidity cause insatiable thirst and water is welcome and refreshing. I do get my eight eight ounce glasses a day now. Something that seems so inconsequential, but is monumentally crucial.

Water also makes me think of other things. I am blessed to have many FB and other friends who are doing great things for God. Some are pastors, some are missionaries, some care for orphans, and many others are using their gifts for the Kingdom each and every day. Sometimes I sit and think of how I would like to do so much for God. I think of orphan children I would like to make sure are fed and loved and know they are special. I would love to tell others the truths He has told me. I would love to pray for others I have never met. God has meant so much to me for over forty years and I wish I could give Him just a fraction of what He has given me. I realize I just have a small life. I wonder what I can do for God?

One day God showed me. I shopped for my brother when he was too weak to shop himself. Without letting him know, I removed those hard to remove covers over the tops of his orange juice and lemonade bottles. You know the ones. I knew he was weak and removing them was difficult for him. One day, he caught me removing the tops. I was expecting him to be uspet because he was very independent. He said, "I forgot to thank you for doing that." I knew he realized I was trying to make things easier for him. Not only did I shop for him, I washed clothes and spent time with him - letting him talk and feel important and valuable. Now, to tell the truth, no one in the world would consider this important, but I think God does. Matthew 10:42 tells us, "... and whoever gives one of these little ones ... even just a cup of cold water because he is My disciple, they will not lose their reward."

A cup of cold water. Everyone can give a cup of cold water. A smile to those around us, a hug to a struggling friend, a cup of tea and company to a widow. An encouraging word to a friend. We all have a cup of cold water. Look for the opportunities every day. I know they are all around. God is watching and He sees everything we do - even if just give a cup of cold water in His Name.

Our friends and family need us to love them and do what we can to make their lives better.

Write about your road and present journey with God. Where are you and where do you want to go?

Day 11 – Value Just Because

A friend once gave me a mug as a gift with the words, "God Danced the Day You Were Born." This gift was meaningful because it came at at time in my life when I was uncertain of my value as a person. The words on the mug were based on the Bible verse, Psalms 139.14 -"I will .... praise You ... for the (awe filled) wonder of my birth!"

The world idolizes fame, fortune and beauty. It makes me wonder exactly what makes us valuable? One of the saddest moments in my life, but should have been one of the happiest, was the day I graduated from veterinary school. I thought this accomplishment would make me feel important and valuable. The truth was when the lights were out and there was no one to pretend to, I felt like a nothing and a nobody. The truth was, I *was* no particular 'body.' I came from a blue collar family that did average jobs and lived in an average neighborhood, and we were unnoticed by others for the most part.

As I struggled with the question, 'was I

valuable', others thought I 'had everything.' I was a registered nurse and just graduated as a veterinarian? They looked at me as if I had the whole world. But deep inside, things were not okay. These things did not make me feel like my life was valuable. Then, the answer came to me from God's Word. The answer is that I am valuable because I am me. Sounds so simple, but I had spent a life time being a 'human-doing' to make myself valuable, when I was a 'human-being' and was valuable to God because I was His and He made me. Human-doings spend their time frantically trying to make themselves approved, lovable, etc. This is exhausting and I don't think it really works. Human-beings are just that - being human.

I know many people who feel their lives are meaningless and some feel worthless. This hurts my heart badly because I felt that way at one time and am blessed to have been able to realize and accept that my Heavenly Father values me above anything monetary on this planet. I am more valuable to Him than all the homes, cars, boats, treasures collected, or anything in this world. He finds me and you HIS most precious possession. (Exodus 19.5)

It matters what we think of ourselves. If we feel our lives are worthless and others' lives are worthless, then we act like it and do self-destructive things or things to hurt others. These only further lead to feelings of worthlessness and it is a vicious cycle. We need to get off the hamster wheel and believe what God has said about us. He loves our brown eyes, blue eyes, curly hair, strait hair, short stature, chubby physique, our sense of humor, and whatever else makes us, us. He danced the day you and I were born. He was there and excited to welcome us to life. He finds us valuable. We do not have to DO anything, all we have to do is BE us.

Yes, I believe we *do* things as Christians in response to the great Love we have received in Jesus, but that is not where our value is, it is just in being us.

My prayer today is for all to know how special and valuable they are.

Write how you are living life to the fullest with God. Are you missing someone? Are you taking all the opportunities presented to do God's work?

_____
_____
_____
_____
_____
_____
_____
_____
_____
_____
_____
_____
_____
_____
_____

Day 12 - Weapons

Could you image a war without any weapons? Kinda comical actually. Sadly, we live in a world inventing more and more devastation producing weapons and every good soldier knows they need weapons. In a perfect world we would never need or use weapons, but in this imperfect world, that will never be. Our enemies will always be prepared for battle.

We not only face the possibility of physical war, we face spiritual war every day. Sometimes we think our battle is against a certain person or circumstance, but there are unseen forces that are against each of us and the ones we love. The Bible tells us this in Ephesians 6.12 - 'For we are not wrestling with flesh and blood [contending only with physical opponents], but against the (tyrannies), against the powers, against [the master spirits who are] the world rulers of this present darkness, against the spirit forces of wickedness in the heavenly (supernatural) sphere.'

In Sun Tzu's well known book, "The Art of

War," he describes many things to prepare for actual war, but I know another Book that tells me the true art of war. Isaiah 54.17 promises believers that 'no weapon forged against you will prevail, and you will refute every tongue that accuses you. This is the heritage of the servants of the Lord, and this is their vindication from Me," declares the Lord.' We are victors in Christ against every attack or unsettling circumstance we face. But we need to be informed.

The Bible assures us - 'For though we walk (live) in the flesh, we are not carrying on our warfare according to the flesh *and* using mere human weapons. For the weapons of our warfare are not physical [weapons of flesh and blood], but they are mighty before God for the overthrow *and* destruction of strongholds.' - 2 Corinthians 10.3-4.

I always wondered exactly what are our weapons? They are prayer, faith, obedience, repentance, praise and worship, the Word of God, the blood of Christ, the Name of Jesus, thanksgiving, the Truth, our salvation, forgiveness, fasting, our confession of our faith and love for God and more. (in no particular order). These are our weapons against defeat, depression, loss of hope, lack of employment, sickness, anything that is against us.

Daniel faithfully prayed three times a day and discovered why there was a delay in the answer. "And [the angel] said to me, O Daniel, you greatly beloved man, understand the words that I speak to you....for to you I am now sent....Then he said to me, Fear not, Daniel, for from the *first day* that you set your mind *and* heart to understand and to humble yourself before your God, your words were heard, and I have come as a consequence of [and in response to] your words. But the prince of the kingdom of Persia withstood me for twenty-one days. Then Michael, one of the chief [of the celestial] princes, came to help me, for I remained there with the kings of Persia." Daniel 10.11-13. Now, I may not know who all the princes and kings are in this passage, but I do know they are enemies and it looks like there was quite a battle before Daniel's prayers were answered.

Ephesians 6.10-18 tells us, 'Finally, be strong in the Lord and in His mighty power. Put on the full armor of God, so that you can take your stand against the devil's schemes...so that when the day of evil comes, you may be able to stand your ground, and after you have done everything, to stand. Stand firm then, with the belt of truth buckled around your waist, with the breastplate of righteousness in place, and with your feet fitted with the readiness that comes from the gospel of peace. In addition to all this, take up the shield of faith, with which you can extinguish all the flaming arrows of the evil one. Take the helmet of salvation and the sword of the Spirit, which is the Word of God. And pray in the Spirit on all occasions with all kinds of prayers and requests. With this in mind, be alert and always keep on praying for all the Lord's people.' Be prepared.

Evil is real and all around, God is real and all around and Greater than anything in the world against us. I John 4.4.

Do you sometimes doubt? Can you write what about? How is God helping with these doubts?
___
___
___
___
___
___
___
___
___
___
___
___
___
___
___
___
___
___
___
___
___
___
___
___

Day 13 - Courage

Even though the truth is I never understood the song "Tin Man" by the music band, 'America,' and the words have some pretty poor grammar, my favorite line is, 'Oz never did given nothin' to the Tin Man that he didn't already have.' I think everyone remembers Dorothy and her three companions going to Oz. Oz really didn't give them anything except the realization of what they already had. The brain, the heart, the courage.

Courage. The Word tells us, 'For God hath not given us the spirit of fear; but of power, and of love, and of a sound mind.' (2 Timothy 1.7.) There is no time for casual faith. The Word tells us, 'The thief comes, to steal, and to kill, and to destroy: I am come that they might have life, and that they might have it more abundantly.' (John 10.10) What thief and what is he stealing?'
The thief is our enemy - the devil. The thief takes our hope, our life, our happiness, our loved ones.. and so on. Jesus came to give life and gave us the power to overcome the evil in our world. Jesus gave us the power to help those around us, but we need

to be aware and we need courage. Abraham had courage. Genesis 14.14-16 says, "When Abraham heard that his nephew had been captured, he armed .... 318 trained servants ...and pursued the enemy....and he brought back all the goods and also brought back his kinsman..and his possessions, the women and ..."

This is one of my favorite examples of a believer hearing his family is in trouble and he 'goes and gets them.' This speaks to me to pray for God to use me to fight the devil (and a great big fight it is sometimes) and 'get my family' back. We are in battle every day. Prayer and putting our faith into action is how we have the courage to rescue our loved ones. Luke 19.46 says, '(Jesus) said to them, "My house will be a house of prayer..." '

It is my heart, and the Heart of the Father, for God to do a miracle for everyone in my family and everyone I meet. Others have tried to convince me that in order for people to have prayers answered, the person being prayed for must be 'willing' to receive a miracle. That may be true and it may not be true. I read in Joshua 2.13, where Rahab asks for her family and states, 'and save alive my father and mother, my brothers and sisters, and all they have and deliver us from death.' AMEN. She prayed for her loved ones and her prayer was answered.

Also in Esther, I see her, her uncle Mordecai, and all the Jews fasting and praying for God to intervene. They were ordinary people who became heroes to those they loved. I am ordinary and believe that for 'such a time as this' (Esther 4.14) God has called me to pray and fast for my kindred and everyone I come in contact with.

The Bible tells of healing that happened when fathers and mothers asked for their children. Jesus did not ask if the recipient was 'willing' to receive. (as in Matthew 8.5-13 as Jesus responded to the Centurion.) This compels me to have courage and be bold in prayer and hold nothing back. It compels me to ask that the ones I love have healthy relationships, be happy in life, be well, have healed hearts and minds, have good lives, strong positive behavior patterns and leave the old destructive lives behind. I pray they be delivered from death. I pray they live and not die because my Savior died for all these things.

These are not the words of lifeless idols, these are the Words of the Living God to us.

Have courage! We have been endowed with it by our Heavenly Father.

Do you have seasons of struggle? Write about it and write if you can ever relate to Job. Do you find others struggling? Do you have hopeful words for them?

_____
_____
_____
_____
_____

Day 14 – Is There a Right Road?

I have heard that 'even atheists pray.' That intrigues me. Why would they pray and who are they praying to? Well known atheist, Christopher Hitchens, wrote a book, "God is not Great." I disagree with his title, but in his book, he outlines how people have claimed to be 'religious' and done unspeakable acts.

While I agree humans are really imperfect, that does not negate the greatness of the Living God to me. He never supported a claim about 'God' not being great, just people. Mr. Hitchens died in December, 2011. I am not 100% certain, but I understand that when his cancer was advancing, he claimed, 'there is much comfort in the old scriptures.' Does perspective change when circumstance changes? Now, Mr. Hitchens knows for certain if there is a God and if there is a heaven, but I would be greatly saddened that with his free will, he chose to not believe.

Another well-known atheist, Stephen Hawking, was claimed to be the smartest man in the world. Mr. Hawking verbally stated he was a godless man. He said all the remarkable things that are true about our bodies and this planet 'are so because they need to be so.' I consider this the most ignorant thing I could ever imagine said, however, what else would a man without God think and say?

I have also heard so many contend that 'all religions' are good. Well, did all the religions have a God that created the universe? or are we still thinking it all came together without any thought or Divine intervention? I am too amazed at Creation to think life just happened to happen. Does it matter what religion we believe? In <u>Joshua 24:15, Joshua</u> states - 'And if it seems evil to you to serve the Lord, choose for yourselves this day whom you will serve, whether the gods which your fathers served on the other side of the River, or the gods of the Amorites, in whose land you dwell; **but as for me and my house, we will serve the Lord**.' Today, the same is true, if other religions are correct, follow them, but as for me and my house, we will serve the Living God, the God of Israel, the God, Jesus, Who died so I can live forever.

Does it really matter what we believe? Jesus tells us in Matthew 7:13 - 'Enter through the narrow gate; for wide is the gate and spacious *and* broad is the way that leads away to destruction, and many are those who are entering through it.' What did He mean? When I look at these Words, they say to me that Jesus is the 'Narrow Gate.' He is the Only Way to life. The wide gate is all the other ways people think they can get to heaven. This is not 'intolerance,' it is the Truth and I believe our very lives depend on it. I believe 'He is the Way, He is the Truth, He is the Life.' (John 14:6)

The next question is always, 'would a 'loving God' punish us?' Deuteronomy 30.19 tells us '(God calls) heaven and earth to witness this day against you that (He has) set before you life and death, the blessings and the curses; therefore choose life..' It appears God allows *us* to make the choice and really wants *us* to make the choice to choose Him.

Yes, I know many 'good' people who even put many Christian believers to shame, but the fact still remains, no one will ever be 'good enough' to get to heaven and the Father without the blood of His Son. We all stand at the foot of the Cross in need of a Savior.

What causes one man to believe so little and another to be so consumed by God? I do not know, but I know I love Him with all my cold little heart is capable of.

Do you have any 'charcoal fires' in your life? If you are not certain, ask God to show you.

_____
_____
_____
_____

Day 15 – The First Thanksgiving

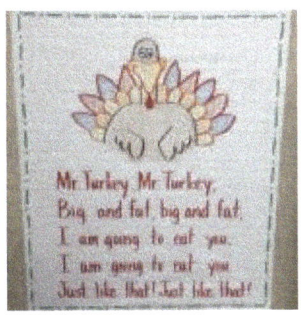

Happy Thanksgiving! Many today with have family and friends over to share a meal and most likely some football!! A day many are off work. Some traveled great distances to celebrate this Thanksgiving 2018. I, myself, traveled from Florida to Ohio. My family is small and we will be going to a restaurant for our meal, but we will be together - laughing and talking for sure.

I remember when I was a little girl, learning of the first Thanksgiving. We were taught about the 'colonists' who were known as Pilgrims. It was in Plymouth. I did not realize at such a young age how brave these travelers were. They left the only home they knew to travel for sixty-six days across a great sea that they may not have made it across. When they did land in America, the land was not welcoming. There were undeveloped areas and some inhospitable people here. They were cold and overcome with disease and loss.

Some Indians were hospitable and taught the newcomers to cultivate corn and make maple syrup. They shared their knowledge and helped them become a part of a new world. I understand our very first Thanksgiving was held by Pilgrims in Wampanoag - no doubt an Indian name - in the Autumn of 1621. This area is now Massachusettes. This day was shared by Pilgrims and the Indians who helped them survive and flourish.

It was not originally a celebration, but a time of prayer. Prayer that allowed the Pilgrims to enjoy their first successful harvest. I cry as I think of how they trusted their God to bless them in this strange and dangerous land. They worked and prayed and when God answered, they were thankful.

In 1863, amid all the goings on with the Civil War, President Lincoln declared the day a National Holiday - again as a day of prayer. President Lincoln stated in a proclamation to all Americans to ask God to 'commend to His tender care all those who have become widows, orphans, mourners, and sufferers in the lamentable civil strife' and the 'heal the wounds of the nation.' Perhaps we need the same prayer today.

Today, many will celebrate with turkey and dressing and pumpkin pie. They will eat so much they will not be able to leave the couch for a while. Not only do I want to enjoy the celebration of the day to give Thanks, but I want to always remember God has blessed me in every way. He has not blessed me to then turn around and think I no longer need Him and no longer need to humble myself to remember all the ways He has produced 'harvest' in my life.

Write your thoughts about heaven.

Day 16 – A Day of Prayer

I understand that it was President Harry Truman that signed a bill into law in 1952 making the National Day of Prayer for America an annual event on the first Thursday of May, encouraging millions across our nation to unite together to pray.

Today is that first Thursday. Now, I realize everyday should be a national day of prayer and a personal day of prayer, but being honest, I find everything in the world to deter me from praying.

I have work and more work, and cooking and caring for others in my life, cleaning the house, taking care of pets, taking the children to every activity they are involved in, even church activities, and television time and more. I am certain everyone can generate a list of all the great reasons why it is difficult to spend time in prayer. I was challenged by a fellow Christian to pray for just *four minutes* a day and have not been able to do that. Four minutes. Sad to admit my failure.

One of my friend's favorite scripture is 1 John 5.14-15 that tells us. "and this is the confidence that we have in Him, that, if we ask any thing according to His will, He hears us: And if we know that He hear us, whatsoever we ask, we know that we have the petitions that we desired of Him." So, the big question is, 'why don't we ask?'

I have a list for that too. Sometimes I doubt, sometimes I am lazy, sometimes I am apathetic, sometimes I think I can manage myself, sometimes I use my busy life as an excuse, and more.

The Word of God is clear that 'the effectual fervent prayer of a righteous man avails much.' James 5.16. I want to make my prayer count and avail much for the ones I see in need. The homeless I pass along the road, the one walking miles down roads that seem to lead no where, the mother's with their children in the grocery store, my family, the young men and women working each day to gain an education or work to make a better life for themselves, family struggling with depression and drug and alcohol addiction, and everyone I meet.

I am always astounded when I read how Jesus' disciples asked Him, 'Teach us to pray' in Luke 11.1. Prayer is something that should come so naturally; something everyone knows how to do. We even see pictures of little children on their knees next to their beds, praying. I do not believe the disciples asked merely to learn how to 'pray' but to 'pray the way He did!' They saw the great works He did and how His life was committed to constant prayer. Amen to that.

Our world is in great need of prayer - from our leaders to our neighbors and families. God is still the answer and He still hears and answers prayers. I do not always pray for my leaders, but God's word teaches us to. 1 Timothy 2.1-2 tells me - 'I exhort therefore, that, first of all, supplications, prayers, intercessions, and giving of thanks, be made for all men; For kings, and for all that are in authority; that we may lead a quiet and peaceable life in all godliness and honesty.'

Join with the nation today and pray.

How can you show patience to others – to family and friends and even strangers?
_____
_____
_____
_____
_____
_____
_____
_____
_____

Day 17 – the Same Spirit

Christ is Risen!

I have read the entire Bible many times. It seems I miss a lot though. One day, while driving, I listened to a minister preaching about the Spirit of God. He mentioned a verse in Romans - 8.11 to be exact - that I have read many times. The verse states "....and if the Spirit of Him who raised Jesus from the dead is living in you...." Either another translation or the minister emphasized this verse to say 'the same Spirit that raised Jesus from the dead is at work in me.' The Words hit me like a ton of bricks. I never noticed these words this way the many times I read my Bible.

The same Spirit - the One that raised Jesus from the dead. God is constantly reminding me of the profound truth and meaning of this verse. I never seem to fully grasp it though. If the same Spirit lives in me, why do I live so below my own expectations? Why do I worry my prayers may not be answered or God may not come through for me?

Why do I think my problems and struggles are too great for the Living God or go unnoticed by Him? Why do I think His love and mercy will end or His supply for my life will end? Why do I go defeated, anxious, and depressed at times?

This season of Jesus' life and death reminds me constantly of the sacrifice my Savior endured so that the same Spirit that raised Him could live in me. The same Spirit that allowed Jesus to cast out demons, heal the sick, raise the dead, and preach the Word. The same Spirit that allows me to be loved by God, be forgiven every weakness and sin, be loved as the imperfect me as God loves Jesus, have everlasting life - here and after physical death, and allows me to pray for the ones I love.

It is the same Spirit that allowed Jesus to turn the water into wine, walk on water, and change His ordinary apostles into committed followers. It is the same Spirt that leads me into truth and truth that allows me to be set free. The same Spirit that is my Comforter, my Counselor, my Way Maker, my Deliverer, my Everything. The same Spirit that was sent from God to me, opened my blind eyes, infills me with power for the tasks of today, and blesses me with assurance of being a child of God. The same Spirit that knows my weaknesses and prays for and through me. The same Spirit that raised Jesus from the dead is at work in me.

I pray for the deep and wonderful revelation of these Words to penetrate every fiber of every readers' being this Lenten season and forever.

Write how you want to see Jesus in the answers when your prayers are answered.

Day 18 - Hypocrite

Sometimes I catch myself saying, "Who am I?" On a good day, I would describe myself as being a pretty good person who is honest and kind and tries to help others as much as I can. I want to 'walk' my 'talk' of Christianity more than anything in this world. Then, sometimes, it seems there is another person living inside me. This other person is impatient, harsh, critical, and more. She comes out at the most surprising moments! Eeeee, how awful. And then, I feel like a hypocrite - one who professes to be something and then, the truth is, is not. Then comes the overwhelming feeling 'I may have to go into hiding."

I am reminded of a precious scripture in Proverbs 24:16 - 'for a righteous man falls seven times and rises...' I ask myself, 'why would a righteous man fall? And why so many times? I feel God responding, 'because he/she is human.' Yes, I am afflicted with the human condition. Is this an excuse? No, not really, but an honest truth. As long as I don human flesh, I will stumble and fall. I will be made to feel as though I have nothing to say because I am imperfect.

The truth is that God knows I am imperfect. It is me that needs to know and realize more clearly each moment of life that grace *is* God's undeserved favor and if I deserved mercy - it would not be mercy. My failure is not bigger than God's love. My true sadness over my mistakes makes me realize the Love I have in my life that is Real and True.

Love - how amazing is it? Well, the Word of God tells us - ' It is because of the Lord's mercy *and* loving-kindness that we are not consumed, because His [tender] compassions fail not. They are new every morning;
great *and* abundant is Your
stability *and* faithfulness.' (Lamentations 3.22-23) My failures bother me, but they do not hinder or lessen the love of God.

Romans 8.38-39 lovingly reminds me '... I am persuaded beyond doubt (am sure) that neither death nor life, nor angels nor principalities, nor things impending *and* threatening, nor things to come, nor powers, nor height nor depth, nor anything else in all creation will be able to separate us from the love of God which is in Christ Jesus our

Lord.' Not even my moments of hypocrisy.

2 Timothy 2.13 assures me, 'If we are faithless [do not believe and are untrue to Him], He remains true (faithful to His Word and His righteous character), for He cannot deny Himself.' It is because Love is patient and kind, keeps no records of wrongs, bears all things, believes all things, hopes all things, endures all things, Love *never* fails and (1 Corinthians 13) God is Love. (1 John 4.8)

I realize I have a huge responsibility to be true to the words God gives me and the life He has entrusted me with, but I am not alone in my shortcomings. Apostle Paul tells us - "For in my inner being I delight in God's law; but I see another law at work in me, waging war against the law of my mind and making me a prisoner of the law of sin at work within me. What a wretched man I am! Who will rescue me from this body that is subject to death?" I am not alone in my struggle to not be a hypocrite.

I not only need to accept God's love and acceptance of me, but I need to forgive myself - even seventy times seven each day. (Matthew 18.22) If I fall, I need to get up, ask for forgiveness, dust myself off, and continue walking with the God I love. Because underneath me are the Everlasting Arms. (Deuteronomy 33.27) FOREVER. The story is about Him. God is the perfect One. Amen.

Write what you find Jesus as – the Lion or the Lamb. Describe why.

Day 19 – Oddly Thankful?

I love roses. Any color, any size, any rose. From the time I see one budding to the unfolding of the petals that seem to be opening to praise God, I love them. There is one thing I don't love about them, though; the thorns.

While reading my little devotional recently, I ran across a little story about a man named George Matheson. Like most of you, I don't know him. I understand he was a blind preacher in Scotland. He was overheard one day telling God that he had thanked Him thousands of times for all the blessings and answered prayers and protection and all that God had done that made him happy - the things he considered 'roses' in his life, but at no time did he thank God for the thorns.

He said he was looking forward to a world where he would be compensated for the cross he bore here on earth, but he never thought of his cross as a present glory from God. He prayed for

God to show him the glory of his cross and the value of his thorn. He prayed for God to show him how he climbed to God through the pathway of his pain and how his tears had made his rainbows.

There are many times I have asked God, "Why?" I thought I could never thank Him for the depression or the anxiety or my constant failures. I thought the low opinion I had for myself could never be used for good in God's Kingdom. I thought I could bear it as He asked me to, but never be truly thankful.

God has miraculously brought me to the place where I can see that He is always faithful and has been my Guide each and every day of my life. He knows every detail about me and the path necessary for me - the path that has led me to know Him in a way I am thoroughly convinced I would never know Him as I do without the pain - without the thorns.

Today I can thank Him for all the pain I have endured, my learning disabilities, my past depression, my past agoraphobia, and even my present anxieties and shortcomings because they keep me connected to Him by reminding me each and every day that I need Him more than I need to take my next breath. How easily I forget sometimes when the thorn is not with me.

The truth is I wish it did not take things that are difficult or painful or sad to make me connect to Him, but He knows how we are as humans. I have others ask me, "Why?" as often as I asked. I do not peddle easy answers to difficult questions, but I always say, "Make your pain your pathway to God." He will be our Everything in everything.

God leads us down every path of our lives and is with us always. His Name is Emmanuel.

Write how you will make the most of each New Year.

Day 20 – What If?

What if we *really* believed? If we really believed everything in God's Word - that He loves us more than anything in this world, that He created us and knows everything about us and truly wants only the best for us? That He is always with us, working for us, and protecting us? Always making ways we could never have imagined? What if He really knows when we are good and when we are not so good and still loves us the same? What if the truth of His Word were not imagination but reality and so much a part of us, nothing could shake it? Would we be different people? I know I would.

Recently I read a short devotional from Joni and friends about Isaiah 49:16 - 'Behold, I have indelibly imprinted (tattooed a picture of) you (engraved you) on the palm of each of My hands..' Joni goes on to write:

"When you were in elementary school, did you ever take a pen and write the name of someone on the palm of your hand? Maybe it was a boy or girl you liked -- or someone you especially admired. The truth is, God has done this as well, only He has taken it a giant step further. In today's Scripture, He says, "See, I have engraved you on the palms of My hands..." In other words, He doesn't just engrave your name on His palms, but He engraves **you**. It's all there -- everything about you -- your hopes and dreams, faults and failures, fears and anxieties, everything that makes up who you are. He's not just holding you; He closes His hands and feels the impression, the precious one-of-a-kind engraving. You are a part of Him, and He will never, ever overlook you and your needs."

This is an amazing truth to me and touches my heart deeply and yet I walk around thinking I am on my own at times - I am sorry to say 'many' times really. I fret and worry and don't know how to pray and all along God is always working on my behalf and always talking. I know in my head that if I really believed all He has said in His Word and to me, I would sleep like a baby every night and smile at everyone every day. I would not be worried about a deal going through for me or if my business will succeed. I would realize God has won the victory for me and rest and enjoy the moments of life He has blessed me with. If only, I say to myself.

In my flawed vision of God, I see Him as asking me to measure up and be something I try to be, but do not seem to be able to be. I do not rest in the Love He has for me. I am asking the Living God to really dwell in me - in every fiber of my being. I want to know that I know that I know He is my God and my Abba Father and that nothing is too trivial for Him and no mistake I make changes His love for me and my family. I want to really experience the empowering Words of the Living God for every part of my life. This is my New Year's resolution after knowing Him for over forty years.

Write how you feel Jesus uses you and if you feel He is able to use you. What are your gifts?

_____
_____
_____
_____
_____
_____
_____
_____
_____
_____
_____
_____
_____

Day 21 – Bella and True Love

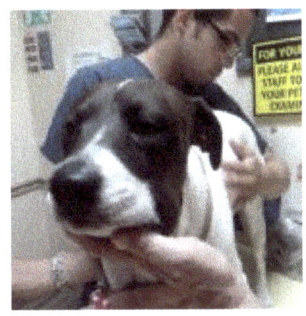

I work at a veterinary clinic near Orlando, Florida. Here is where I met Bella. It seemed a routine recheck for a dog that had been bitten by a rattlesnake three days earlier and taken to a local emergency clinic for care. There she received two units of antivenin and her blood work was assessed to make certain the effects of the poison interfering with her ability to clot her blood were no longer a threat.

Snakes are a serious threat in Florida and may be seen in plain view anywhere, anytime. I read the emergency clinic report dutifully and did my exam. Bella was bitten in the facial area - the swelling can be seen under her left ear. I informed the owner of the resulting wounds that would most likely occur because of the poison and the care they may require. Snake bites are deceptively small, but the danger is huge and the resulting damage to the tissues affected by the poison can be quite extensive. She said she would do *anything* necessary to save her dog. Then I began to cry.

Bella's owner shared the details of the incident. Bella was was bitten because the rattlesnake - not a pygmy rattler, but a BIG rattlesnake with SEVEN rattles the owner said - was actually striking at her. Bella, sensing danger, put herself in harms way to protect her owner and took the bite. My heart melted as I stroked Bella's face and told her what a very good girl she is. She gave me kisses as her owner and I continued our talk.

What a remarkable story. A loyal dog saved her owner and now a loyal owner is determined to save her dog. Hats off to all the great dogs in the world and especially to Bella!

This story reminds me how my Savior knew the danger I faced and He took all of the danger for me to live. It may not have been a 'snake bite,' but my Savior did put Himself in harm's way to save me. He died on a Cross so I do not have to die and I do not need to save Him back, but have dedicated my life to sharing His Good News with everyone I meet.

Hebrews 2.9 reminds me - "but we see Jesus, who was made a little lower than the angels for the suffering of death, crowned with glory and honor; that He by the grace of God should taste death for every man." "Thanks be unto God for his unspeakable Gift! " 2 Corinthians 9.15.

Write how you think Jesus sees you. Do you feel valuable to Him? Do you need candles lit?

_____
_____
_____
_____
_____
_____
_____
_____
_____
_____
_____
_____
_____
_____
_____
_____
_____
_____
_____
_____
_____
_____
_____
_____

Day 22 - Signs

I love rainbows. Every time I get in a jam or confused about life and feel like I really need a sign He is still there, it seems God manages to put a rainbow in the sky. This is absolutely true - He even put them in the Ohio sky when it was not even raining!

I guess if I had great faith, I would never need a sign, but sometimes I do and sometimes I ask for one. I just want to know it is Him and not me and my crazy imaginations. The Bible tells me of those who also wanted a sign - like Gideon in Judges 6.17 - 'Gideon said to Him, If now I have found favor in Your sight, then show me a sign that it is You Who talks with me.'

Even Hezekiah asked for a sign - "Hezekiah said to Isaiah, What shall be the sign that the Lord will heal me and that I shall go up into the house of the Lord on the third day?" 1 Kings 20.8

I believe if we need a sign, He will give us one, but I also believe that the 'signs' are truly all around us. For instance, the sun came up again today, gravity is still holding us on the planet, the birds are still singing, the whales are in their ocean, the fruit trees are still producing luscious fruit, gardens are still producing abundant crops from mere seeds, babies are still being born, little bees are still making honey, and He's still talking to us and more!

I admit I falter in faith at times, one of my favorite passages in the Bible is about Paul and the ones he's traveling with -

"20 And when neither sun nor stars were visible for many days and no small tempest kept raging about us, all hope of our being saved was finally abandoned.

21 Then as they had eaten nothing for a long time, Paul came forward into their midst and said, Men, you should have listened to me, and should not have put to sea from Crete and brought on this disaster and harm *and* misery *and* loss.

22 But [even] now I beg you to be in good spirits *and* take heart, for there will be no loss of life among you but only of the ship.

23 For this [very] night there stood by my side an angel of the God to Whom I belong and Whom I serve *and* worship,

24 And he said, Do not be frightened, Paul! It is necessary for you to stand before Caesar; and behold, God has given you all those who are sailing with you." Acts 27.20-24. And all those who are sailing with us!

I wish I could always say, "God said, I believe." Very simple, but I am working on it.

The signs of Him are all around us and if we need one more or two more or three more, I believe He will give them to us. He wants us to know that we know that we know He is real and Who and What He says He is in His Word.

Write how you want to make Thanksgiving something to do every day.

_____
_____
_____
_____
_____
_____
_____
_____
_____
_____
_____
_____
_____

Day 23 – He Left Them

It must have been remarkable to see Jesus after thinking He was not alive any longer. Witnessing the brutal treatment and crucifixion had to be devastating. The Bible tells us He appeared to His disciples and many others after He rose from the dead, but after forty days, He ascended into heaven. He left them - again. But this time, not without leaving them the promised Holy Spirit.

Jesus assured them, "I will not leave you as orphans [comfortless, desolate, bereaved, forlorn, helpless]; I will come [back] to you." (John 14.18)

The Holy Spirit is part of the Trinity, but it seems I don't hear much about the Holy Spirit. In fact, some others never heard of Him as I read Acts 19.2 - "...and he asked them, Did you receive the Holy Spirit when you believed [on Jesus as the Christ]? And they said, No, we have not even heard that there is a Holy Spirit."

The Holy Spirit is a free gift - "If you ... know how to give good gifts ...to your children, how much more will your heavenly Father give the Holy Spirit to those who ask *and* continue to ask Him!" (Luke 11.13)

What does the Holy Spirit help us with?

1. **Hope and love** - "Such hope never disappoints *or* deludes *or* shames us, for God's love has been poured out in our hearts through the Holy Spirit Who has been given to us. (Romans 5.5)

2. **Freedom from condemnation** "For the law of the Spirit of life [which is] in Christ Jesus [the law of our new being] has freed me from the law of sin and of death." (Romans 8.2)

3. **Comforter, Helper, Counselor, Intercessor, Advocate, Standby, Teacher** - "but the Comforter (Counselor, Helper, Intercessor, Advocate, Strengthener, Standby), the Holy Spirit, Whom the Father will send in My name [in My place, to represent Me and act on My behalf], He will teach you all things." (John 14.26)

4. **Prayer Partner** - "So too the [Holy] Spirit comes to our aid *and* bears us up in our weakness; for we do not know what prayer to offer *nor* how to offer it

worthily as we ought, but the Spirit Himself goes to meet our supplication *and* pleads in our behalf with unspeakable yearnings *and* groaninga too deep for utterance. (Romans 8.26)

5. **Infuser of Power** - "but you shall receive power (ability, efficiency, and might) when the Holy Spirit has come upon you, and you shall be My witnesses....to the ends (the very bounds) of the earth." (Acts 1.8)

6. **Gifts of faith and healing** - "to another [wonder-working] faith by the same [Holy] Spirit, to another the extraordinary powers of healing by the one Spirit.." (1 Corinthians 12.9)

7. **Allows us access to the Father** - "For it is through Him that we ...have ....access by one [Holy] Spirit to the Father [so that we are able to approach Him]. (Ephesians 2.18)

8. **Keeps us and guards us** - "Guard *and* keep [with the greatest care] the precious *and* excellently adapted [Truth] which has been entrusted [to you], by the [help of the] Holy Spirit Who makes His home in us. (2 Timothy 1.14)

and more!

The Holy Spirit is Great Gift to us by the Father Who wants to make His home in us. I always ask to see all Three in the Trinity more clearly and reap the benefits of the sacrifice of my Savior.

Write how you feel Jesus wants you to feel about others and how you do feel about them.

Day 24 - Peace

I understand that when a hurricane comes, birds instinctively find the 'eye' of the storm. I have been told that skies are often clear above the eye and winds are relatively light because it is actually the calmest section of any hurricane. The eye is so calm because the strong surface winds that converge towards the center never reach it. Smart little winged creatures! They travel within the eye.

Recently, I have enjoyed finding a place of rest in the midst of what in past times in life would have been overwhelming to me. I am not by nature a calm person. I wonder how I have lived so many years without true peace? I do not know why I have been so anxious in life, however, this seems to be a season in my life that *finally* the truth of God's Words is penetrating in a real and deep way. It has not come easily though, I have be honest.

A truth in the Bible hit me like a ton of bricks

the other day. Jesus *gives* us His peace.

"Peace I leave with you; My [own] peace I now give *and* bequeath to you. Not as the world gives do I give to you. Do not let your hearts be troubled, neither let them be afraid. [Stop allowing yourselves to be agitated and disturbed; and do not permit yourselves to be fearful and intimidated and cowardly and unsettled.]" John 14.27.

I must have read this verse hundreds, if not thousands, of times over the 45 years I have read the Bible. But I never had true peace. I pretended to and wished I had, but the truth is , I had turmoil, anxiety, worry, and more. I bragged about making worrying an Olympic sport. Very foolish really.

Peace- I cannot even grasp the true meaning of the word or find words to define 'peace.' Free of anxiety, tranquil, no emotional upset, and other words may be available, but not truly express the still feeling that is glorious deep inside oneself that is called 'peace.' This is what God wants for us and God gives to us - as a free gift.

God's Word also tells us, "Do not fret *or* have any anxiety about anything, but in every circumstance *and* in everything, by prayer and petition ([a]definite requests), with thanksgiving, continue to make your wants known to God. And *God's peace* [shall be yours, that [b]tranquil state of a soul assured of its salvation through Christ, and so fearing nothing from God and being content with its earthly lot of whatever sort that is, that peace] which *transcends all understanding* shall [c]garrison *and* mount guard over your hearts and minds in Christ Jesus. Philippians 4.6-7. (emphasis mine) Another version calls it 'the peace that passes understanding."

I pray for you and all of the ones you love to be blessed in a new way today with God's peace.

Write your inner thoughts and struggles. Take them to Jesus for His care and help.

___
___
___
___
___
___
___
___
___
___
___
___
___
___
___
___
___
___
___
___
___
___
___
___

Day 25 - ...and we did not care..

I am not sure I have heard sadder words than, "I don't care" or "who cares?" How important is it to care?

I once heard a young man talking about his relationship with his father. To be honest, his father seemed harsh in his punishment for the things this young man did wrongly. After a number of years of wrongdoing and being punished, the young man was arrested. His father never punished him for this. The young man was confused and asked why? and his father said, "I just don't care anymore."

According to the young man, this small, but powerful statement hurt that young man more than all the excessive punishment he had received in the past. For someone to 'not care' who was inherently supposed to care was apparently devastating to him.

I have contemplated the words of this young man many times. What and who do I care about? I care about eating and sleeping and exercising and working. I care about my clients and pets. Do I care about my neighbor or family or co-workers? I hope I do.

Some tragic events in the Bible talk about Jesus and caring. The New Living Translation Bible quotes Isaiah 53.3 as "He was despised and rejected—a man of sorrows, acquainted with deepest grief. We turned our backs on him and looked the other way. He was despised, and we did not care."

Tragic words to me. The Creator of the Universe, the Eternal One, Almighty God came from heaven, became a man, walked among us, did many miracles, taught God's Words, never hurt anyone, was tortured, and 'we did not care.'

I realize many do care, but there are many that do not take notice of the profound and ultimate Gift God has given to us and the true impact of the Cross and Jesus' life and sacrifice.

Matthew 22 tells me another tragic story - "Jesus spoke to them again in parables, saying: "The kingdom of heaven is like a king who prepared a wedding banquet for his son. He sent his servants to those who had been invited to the banquet to tell them to come, but they refused to come....." Some had other things they considered more important - they plowed fields, married off their children, and more. They had no time for God.

Because of this Lenten season we celebrate - the life and death of Jesus - and His resurrection, we have all been invited to the banquet. It is a season for caring.

I love Lionel Harris' song - "He paid too high a price to have my soul just stirred at times, but never really changed...."

I pray for everyone to care.

Write how your love meter is doing.

_____
_____
_____
_____
_____
_____
_____
_____
_____
_____
_____
_____
_____
_____
_____

Day 26 – Que Sera, Sera

I, like just about everyone I know, would love to know the future. I sit and wonder if I will ever own a home? if I will own a horse again? if I will ever fall in love? will my anxiety and sadness at times ever go away for good? Sometimes I tease about 'being psychic,' but it just ain't so. So many say we would really *not* want to see into the future, but sometimes just a quick glimpse of a certain present circumstance outcome seems like it would be nice.

The truth is that many times I rob myself of the joy of the moments I have being so preoccupied with all the tomorrows of my life. Jesus told us not to be worried about tomorrow when He said 'So do not worry *or* be anxious about tomorrow, for tomorrow will have worries *and* anxieties of its own. Sufficient for each day is its own trouble.' Matthew 6.34. Yes, tomorrow will have a whole new set of challenges and problems and the God we love will not be scrambling around trying to figure out how to help us. So, I need to stick to today.

Recently, I encountered a situation that has caused me much grief. I did not know which way to turn. Some things pointed to my staying and seeing what happened, and some things pointed to the situation being hopeless and my need to run away from the situation as fast as I possibly could. What to do? Well, I decided to jump ship. I can't say I have not been confused and disappointed. Why did this happen to begin with? It seems like such an experience in futility to be honest.

While reading my devotions one day, I came across Matthew 24.1-2 -'Jesus departed from the temple area and was going on His way when His disciples came up to Him to call His attention to the buildings of the temple *and* point them out to Him. But He answered them, Do you see all these? Truly I tell you, there will not be left here one stone upon another that will not be thrown down.' It hit me like a ton of bricks. My Savior knows all about the future. Every minute of my future, your future, our futures.

When I am disappointed, I lose site of this fact. I lose site of the fact I can trust the Man Who died for me to know all about my future and all about what is good and not good for me. I can trust Him to direct all my steps even when I cry myself to sleep wondering why something did not turn out as I had hoped.

My faith seems like imagination more times than I wish, but after all the wrestling and struggling through everything, God makes His Light to shine on the situation and I want to trust Him. I want to love Him even when I do not understand because I know that I know that I know, He does and does want what is best for me.

Write how you see Jesus sees you and the ones you Do you find Him in everything?

_____
_____
_____
_____
_____
_____
_____
_____
_____
_____
_____
_____
_____
_____
_____
_____
_____
_____
_____
_____
_____

Day 27 – Hosana

Hosanna!

A shout of praise or adoration; an acclamation. I feel praise is the offering of grateful respect or reverence that is rendered in words or song; as an act of worship. The crowd cried Hosanna in the streets on what we celebrate this Sunday as Palm Sunday.

Most know the story of Jesus riding through the streets on a donkey being praised and adored; palm branches lining the streets. Matthew 21.9 tells us 'And the multitudes that went before, and that followed, cried, saying, Hosanna to the son of David: Blessed is He that comes in the name of the Lord; Hosanna in the highest.' In Luke 19.39-40, the story continues how the religious leaders tried to stop the praise - "some of the Pharisees in the crowd said to Jesus, 'Teacher, rebuke your disciples!' to which Jesus replied 'I tell you, if they keep quiet, the stones will cry out.'" Creation praises God every moment. So will I.

The greatest adoration for our God is to praise Him. Praise flows from a grateful heart and demonstrates our love for God. In fact, praise is one of the greatest weapons against attacks of the enemy. The gates of hell cannot resist against our worship and praise. The devil is no match for the praise we give to God. I have experienced relief from tormenting anxiety and depression if I just sing a song of praise to the God I love.

The account of Paul and Silas being imprisoned shows how mighty our praise to God is - "..but about midnight, as Paul and Silas were praying and singing hymns of praise to God, and the [other] prisoners were listening to them, suddenly there was a great earthquake, so that the very foundations of the prison were shaken; and at once all the doors were opened and everyone's shackles were unfastened." Acts 16.25-26. Our chains also come loose and we cannot be stopped in any way from healing, restoration, financial blessing, answered prayers, freedom from addictions, depression, and other tormenting things around us. Praise is powerful.

Psalms mentions praising God at least 150 times and I find Psalm 150 tells us best -

Praise the Lord. Praise God in His sanctuary;

 Praise Him in His mighty heavens.

Praise Him for His acts of power;

Praise Him for His surpassing greatness.

Praise Him with the sounding of the trumpet,

Praise Him with the harp and lyre,

Praise Him with timbrel and dancing

Praise Him with the strings and pipe,

Praise Him with the clash of cymbals

Praise Him with resounding cymbals.

Let everything that has breath praise the Lord. AMEN

Happy Palm Sunday everyone.

Write how you feel Jesus has given you friends and made life easier.

_____
_____
_____
_____
_____
_____
_____
_____

Day 28 – First Choice

Sometimes I think I have more challenges than I can handle and I frequently wonder why difficult things happen. I do not think I am alone in wondering.

Everyone who knows me knows that CS Lewis is one of my favorite authors. I recently discovered a new blurb of his. I have never been in country at war and this is from a collection of his letters to others about war time- TO BEDE GRIFFITHS: *On fortitude and trust in God in the face of war; and on ecumenical differences* dated 29 April 1938:

"I have been in considerable trouble over the present danger of war. Twice in one life—and then to find how little I have grown in fortitude despite my conversion. It has done me a lot of good by making me realise how much of my happiness secretly depended on the tacit assumption of at least tolerable conditions for the body: and I see more clearly, I think, the necessity (if one may so put it) which God is under of allowing us to be afflicted—so few of us will *really* rest all on Him if He leaves us any other support."

What he writes rings true with me. I want to be comfortable and much of my happiness depends on it. To tell the truth, if I was not forced to depend on Him, I am not certain I would. Sad though, really. Why is this so?

I ask myself this question daily. Is He my First Choice? What is the Bible filled with? The answer is - God's love for us, His faithfulness, His ability, His all knowing and all seeing, His care, His desire to answer prayer, His wanting us to see Him as He is and not as we are - broken, frail - and His true desire to have us trust Him with everything every moment.

Is 40.26 reminds me "Lift up your eyes and look to the heavens: Who created all these?

He who brings out the starry host one by one and calls forth each of them by name. Because of his great power and mighty strength, not one of them is missing."

The God that named the stars and keeps them, keeps me and all that concerns me.

Romans 8.15 tells me "the Spirit you received does not make you slaves, so that you live in fear again; rather, the Spirit you received brought about your adoption to sonship. And by him we cry, '*Abba,* Father.'" Abba is a very tender word that means 'daddy.'

There isn't enough paper to add how Jesus says He is my Shepherd, He is the Truth, the Way, the Light, the Bread, the Eternal One, the Living Water, the Resurrection, Counselor, Prince of Peace, Wonderful. He is Everything.

He has called me by my name and knows every detail about me and my life and what has hurt and what has made me happy and will make me happy. He reminds me "the earth is the Lord's and everything in it, the world, and all who live in it..." Psalm 24.1. He owns all the animals in the forest and all the cattle on a thousand hills. Psalm 50.10. And He tells us how He gives us great and precious promises to care for us and love us.

This means He owns all the jobs, all the money in the world, all the homes, all the physical things and spiritual things available to us. He gives us all things through Christ.

To tell the truth, what more could I ever want? Why would I go to any other source for anything when He never runs out of anything. He never runs out of patience with me and for that I am eternally grateful to Him. I want to make Him my First Choice in every situation.

Write how you use your words.

Day 29 - Headlines

Today's headlines are sometimes very shocking:

Volcanic Eruption in Yellowstone to Devastate All of America!

Two Americans Slain on Vacation!

Is the Pilot Intoxicated?

Politicians Tell Poor to Riot and 'Just Steal the Food'!

Young Men Accused of Stabbing French Policeman!

Korea Testing Nuclear Weapons!

Middle East Shooting Down Drones!

Gas Prices Rising!

Drought/Fire/Rain Ravishing Homes and Farmland - Food Prices Will be Higher!

Another Earthquake Hits California!

I have been inundated with troublesome news, but THESE are a few of God's Headlines:

"...God will liberally supply (fill to the full) your every need according to His riches in glory in Christ Jesus." (Philippians 4.19)

"greater is He that is in you, than he that is in the world." (1 John 4.4)

"thanks be to God, Who gives us the victory through our Lord Jesus Christ." (1 Corinthians 15.57)

"For God so loved the world, He gave His Only Son, that whoever believes on Him will never perish, but have everlasting life." (John 3.16)

"..thanks be unto God, Who always causes us to triumph in Christ." (2 Corinthians 2.14)

"..no weapon that is formed against you shall prosper, and every tongue that shall rise against you in judgment you shall show to be in the wrong. This [peace, righteousness, security, triumph over opposition] is the heritage of the servants of the Lord." (Isaiah 54.17)

"there is no Rock like our God." (I Samuel 2.2)

"...and surely I am with you always, to the very end of the age." (Matthew 28.20)

"I have told you these things, so that in Me you may

have [perfect] peace *and* confidence. In the world you have tribulation *and* trials *and* distress *and* frustration; but be of good cheer [take courage; be confident, certain, undaunted]! For I have overcome the world. [I have deprived it of power to harm you and have conquered it for you.]" (John 16.33)

I am the Alpha and the Omega, the First and the Last (the Before all and the End of all). (Revelation 22.13)

"The seventh angel sounded his trumpet, and there were loud voices in heaven, which said: 'The kingdom of the world has become the kingdom of our God and of His Christ, and He shall reign for ever and ever.'" (Revelation 11.15)

I am certain you know more of God's great headlines.

Amen to God's Headlines.

Write how you approach God with your needs.

_____
_____
_____
_____
_____
_____
_____

Day 30 - More

The concept of more is not a new one. I used to want more and more. I even had people calling me to offer me more - more furniture, more add ons to my home, more, more, more.

I guess it is old age because I have come to a time where I do not want more *things*. But I definitely want more. I want more patience that takes away worry, weeping, self-works, want, weakening, and wobbling. I want more of His Word in my heart helping me "Rest in the Lord, and wait patiently for Him." Psalm 37.7

I want more revelation - "That the God of our Lord Jesus Christ, the Father of glory, may give unto (me) the spirit of wisdom and revelation in the knowledge of Him: The eyes of (my) understanding being enlightened; that (I) may know what is the hope of His calling, and what the riches of the glory of His inheritance in the saints, And what is the exceeding greatness of his power to (me) who believe(s), according to the working of His mighty power." Ephesians 1.17-19

I want more healing - "..but he was wounded for our transgressions, he was bruised for our iniquities: the chastisement of our peace was upon him; and with his stripes we are healed." Isaiah 53.5

I want more peace - "Do not fret *or* have any anxiety about anything, but in every circumstance *and* in everything, by prayer and petition (definite requests), with thanksgiving, continue to make your wants known to God. And God's peace [shall be yours, that [b]tranquil state of a soul assured of its salvation through Christ, and so fearing nothing from God and being content with its earthly lot of whatever sort that is, that peace] which transcends all understanding shall [c]garrison *and* mount guard over your hearts and minds in Christ Jesus. Philippians 4.6-7.

I want more faith - "Now faith is the assurance (the confirmation, (the title deed) of the things [we] hope for, being the proof of things [we] do not see *and* the conviction of their reality [faith perceiving as real fact what is not revealed to the senses]. Hebrews 11.1 and the whole chapter.

I want more works for God - "..and I by [good] works [of obedience] will show you my faith." James 2.18

I want more victory - "But thanks be to God, Who gives us the victory [making us conquerors] through our Lord Jesus Christ." 1 Corinthians 15.57

I want more joy - "And be not grieved *and* depressed, for the joy of the Lord is your strength *and* stronghold." Nehemiah 8.10.

I want more worship - "...let us therefore, receiving a kingdom that is
firm *and* stable *and* cannot be shaken, offer to God pleasing service *and* acceptable worship, with modesty *and* pious care and godly
fear *and* awe..." Hebrews 12:28

I want more long- suffering - " But we commend ourselves in every way as [true] servants of God: through great endurance, in
tribulation *and* suffering, in
hardships *and* privations, in sore
straits *and* calamities,..." 2 Corinthians 6

I want more kindness - "..love is kind"- 1 Corinthians 13.4

I want more wisdom - "If any of you lack wisdom, let him ask of the giving God [Who gives] to everyone .... and it will be given him." James 1.5

Yes, I think I am guilty. I want more, Lord. In Jesus' Name. Amen.

Share your stories with us.

Write about a superhero you know. Are you a superhero to someone?

Day 31 – More on More

    I adore Anne Klein clothes. I bought a beautiful skirt by her once. After bringing it home, I had second thoughts, so I drove back to the store to return my purchase. The clerk asked if there was anything wrong with the skirt. I replied, "No." She then asked if it looked okay - which I replied, "It is lovely." When she began to ask a third question, I stopped her mid sentence and tensely stated, "I have a shopping problem, can you please just take the skirt back." She did so without any further interrogation.

    I have given up wanting 'more' things, but not more of God. To continue my list from last week, I do want more, much more.

I want more blessing - "The blessing of the Lord, it makes (us) rich, and He adds no sorrow with it." Proverbs 10.22

I want more favor - "You open Your hand and satisfy

every living thing with favor." Psalm 145.16

I want more answers to prayer - "The earnest (heartfelt, continued) prayer of a righteous man makes tremendous power available [dynamic in its working]." James 5.16 b

I want a more of a closer walk with God - "Come close to God and He will come close to you." James 4.8

I want more inspiration - "..but they were not able to resist the intelligence *and* the wisdom and [the inspiration of] the Spirit with which *and* by Whom he spoke." Acts 6.10

I want more purity - "With the pure You will show Yourself pure." Psalm 18.26

I want more holiness - "...but as the One Who called you is Holy, you yourselves also be holy in all your conduct *and* manner of living." 1 Peter 1.15

I want to be more obedient - "..and now, what does the Lord your God ask of you but to fear the Lord your God, to walk in obedience to Him, to love Him, to serve the Lord your God with all your heart and with all your soul" Deuteronomy 10.12

I want more teaching - "(My) God instructs (me) and teaches (me) the right way." Isaiah 28.26

I want more of His Word - "Your word is a lamp for my feet, a light on my path." Psalm 119.105

I want more direction -
"The steps of a good man are ordered by the Lord: and he delighteth in his way." Psalm 37.23

I want more good fruit - "For every tree is known by his own fruit." Luke 6.44 and "... the fruit of the Spirit is love, joy, peace, longsuffering, gentleness, goodness, faith, Meekness, temperance: against such there is no law." Galatians 5.22-23

I want more reverence - "Wherefore, we receiving a kingdom which cannot be moved, let us have grace, whereby we may serve God acceptably with reverence and godly fear." Hebrews 12.28

Yes, I am still guilty of greed and wanting more. God bless everyone.

Share what Easter means to you and how you remember the Cross each day.

_____
_____
_____
_____
_____
_____
_____
_____
_____
_____
_____
_____

Bonus Day – Great Reward

I am still of the age that I need to work. It is a bummer, but I am grateful to have work and God blesses me tremendously. I am 'rewarded' well for my efforts.

In life, I want other rewards too sometimes. I have the mentality that when I do something good, I should be rewarded. The 'karma' thing. Do good - good comes back, do bad - and, you know. I have come to realize that this does not always work this way. Sometimes you just have to reconcile to do good because it is the right thing to do, God has commanded us to, and this is really the people we want to be. The good thing is its own reward. God promises to reward us though - "he who sows righteousness (moral and spiritual rectitude in every area and relation) shall have a sure reward [permanent and satisfying]." (Proverbs 11.18)

Sometime I wonder what my 'reward' will be at the end of life? I know I will be in heaven with Jesus and those I love. Will I have a mansion in Glory? Will the good deeds I did on Earth be noticed and the times I fell short not diminish the end result of a life lived? Jesus promises rewards - "for the Son of Man is going to come in the glory (majesty, splendor) of His Father with His angels, and then He will render account *and* reward every man in accordance with what he has done." (Matthew 16.27)

When I arrive in heaven, I want God to say, 'Welcome, good and faithful servant.' I have the image of casting my crown at the feet of Jesus - Who washed the feet of His disciples to demonstrate how we should treat others. I have a vision of walking streets of gold and never crying again, never feeling sad or lonely, never having another worry. I have hope of seeing everyone I have loved and even seeing the animals God gave me to love here. After all, He placed more animals on the Ark than people, so their Creator is my Creator and I know He loves the animals too.

But the most important and precious Reward I have ever received in my life is God, Himself. God told Abraham He would be his Great Reward - "after these things the Word of the Lord came unto Abram in a vision, saying, Fear not, Abram: I am thy

Shield, and thy exceeding great Reward." (Genesis 15.1)

I used to be upset about this. I wanted a family and financial success and 'other things,' just more 'things.' Now, I humbly tell God with a grateful heart how much I love Him and am so happy He pursued me and saved me and has walked with me all these years of life and never let me down. How could I have ever thought anything on this Earth could be more valuable to me than God?

He is my Great Reward and it has been the best Reward I could have ever imagined. Being a child of the Living God - I almost can't believe it because it is so great.

Write if you feel broken at times. Write how you respond to others who are broken.

_____
_____
_____
_____
_____
_____
_____
_____
_____
_____

Bonus Day – So Will I

My sincere prayer for Ash Wednesday:

God of creation
There at the start
Before the beginning of time
With no point of reference
You spoke to the dark
And fleshed out the wonder of light
And as You speak
A hundred billion galaxies are born
In the vapor of Your breath the planets form
If the stars were made to worship so will I

I can see Your heart in everything You've made
Every burning star
A signal fire of grace
If creation sings Your praises so will I

God of Your promise
You don't speak in vain
No syllable empty or void
For once You have spoken
All nature and science
Follow the sound of Your voice

And as You speak
A hundred billion creatures catch Your breath
Evolving in pursuit of what You said
If it all reveals Your nature so will I

I can see Your heart in everything You say
Every painted sky
A canvas of Your grace
If creation still obeys You so will I
So will I
So will I

If the stars were made to worship so will I
If the mountains bow in reverence so will I
If the oceans roar Your greatness so will I
For if everything exists to lift You high so will I
If the wind goes where You send it so will I
If the rocks cry out in silence so will I

If the sum of all our praises still falls shy
Then we'll sing again a hundred billion times

God of salvation
You chased down my heart
Through all of my failure and pride
On a hill You created
The Light of the world
Abandoned in darkness to die

And as You speak
A hundred billion failures disappear
Where You lost Your life so I could find it here
If You left the grave behind You so will I

I can see Your heart in everything You've done
Every part designed in a work of art called love
If You gladly chose surrender so will I

I can see Your heart
Eight billion different ways
Every precious one
A child You died to save
If You gave Your life to love them so will I

Like You would again a hundred billion times
But what measure could amount to Your desire
You're the One who never leaves the one behind

Amen.

Write your thoughts about your devotion to God.
_____
_____
_____
_____
_____
_____
_____
_____
_____
_____
_____
_____
_____
_____
_____
_____

www.ingramcontent.com/pod-product-compliance
Lightning Source LLC
Chambersburg PA
CBHW041318110526
44591CB00021B/2823